A PRIMER ON DISPENSATIONALISM

by

John H. Gerstner

ISBN: 0-87552-273-4

Printed in the United States of America

DEDICATION

To Lillian Love,
Anti-antinomian

PREFACE

This elementary presentation focuses on several crucial features of dispensationalism in its classic form, "Scofieldism."

Changes are taking place in that theology, and most of them are changes for the better. For example, regarding the Scofield Bible's view that the Holy Spirit did not regenerate the Old Testament people of God (compare the note on Zech. 12:10), a number of dispensationalists are coming to a better view (even among the editors of the Scofield Bible itself).

Yet, these changes (which I most cordially welcome) are not fundamental and systematic. They represent a tendency but not a clear and clean break with the abominable heresy of antinomianism, which is endemic to dispensationalism.

I am certain that, if and when such a break occurs, those who are part of it will eagerly and candidly distance themselves from their former, dispensational views, whatever the cost. It is my hope that this primer will spur them lovingly in that direction.

I owe my salvation, under God, to a dispensationalist. When I came to the Philadelphia School of the Bible, in 1932, I was a professing Christian, but I did not really understand the way of salvation. The most crucial half-hour in my entire life began when I asked the Dean of that school, the rather silly question, "What do you teach here?" He felt a question like that deserved the full treatment. For half an hour, he told me what the Philadelphia School of the Bible taught, while I stood there transfixed. Although I had known something about Christ and His death, not until that moment did I understand that He died for the remission of our sins and that the whole Bible from beginning to end was the telling of that wonderful story. My gratitude to that teacher, and to the whole dispensational school of theology which he represented, will linger with me through eternity.

Nevertheless, I believe the theology of dispensationalism, though intending evangelicalism, is a serious deviation from biblical doctrine and even threatens its own evangelicalism. This primer will try to show the truth of that heavy charge. I show my gratitude to all dispensationalists by attempting to correct the errors I see in their system. My heart is sad to say these things; but, as God is my witness, it is a deep labor of love on my part. Never did anybody feel more affection for a group of people whom he had to criticize than I feel for dispensationalists, past and present.

THE FUNDAMENTAL IDEA:
DIVIDING RATHER THAN UNIFYING THE BIBLE

A central text of the dispensational theology is II Timothy 2:15, "Study to show thyself approved unto God, a workman that needeth not to be ashamed, rightly dividing the word of truth." (See C. I. Scofield's comment on this verse in his work *Rightly Dividing the Word of Truth.)*

From the beginning, dispensationalists have interpreted this statement to mean that the Bible is presented in sharply divided parts called dispensations. Correctly interpreting the Bible is correctly dividing these dispensations from one another.

In itself, that is not an erroneous opinion. Paul's word *oikonomia* means administration and implies discerning or distinguishing the differences in the various periods of biblical revelation, as the Criswell Study Bible states, it is "the plain, straightforward understanding of the Scripture. . . ." The church has so understood it through the ages. What is peculiar about the dispensational way of understanding is not its seeing different, unfolding stages of revelation but the way it sees those stages. Unlike traditional interpreters, dispensationalists "divide" these sections sharply into areas that *conflict with* one another rather than *unfold from* one another. Genuine biblical revelation is developmental; one stage unfolds naturally from another as the unfolding of the blossom of a flower. But for dispensationalists, these periods are sharply divided rather than integrated, and they conflict rather than harmonize. Even "divide" is a sharper term than Paul's original requires, and dispensationalists have made it sharper still, a veritable scissor separation of one part from another.

Oswald Allis has noted that feature. As an Old Testament scholar, he was impressed with dispensationalism's similarity to radical biblical criticism. Dispensationalists are generally very conservative and anti-critical. They all agree that the Bible is the Word of God, unlike the Bible critic who assumes it is a mere product of men. Consequently, Allis notes with surprise that these ultra-conservatives and ultra-radicals close ranks by the radical way they cut up the Bible. Radical scholars divide the Old Testament into different and conflicting documents with varying theologies. Dispensationalists do not go about their job in quite the same way, but they end up with very similar results. Just as there are radical radicals who split the biblical documents to smithereens, so there are ultra-dispensationalists (Bullingerites) who do the same.

As we shall see throughout this booklet, the dispensational interpretations resulting from such radical divisions of the biblical revelation are unjustified.

Generally speaking, dispensationalists consider themselves much more loyal than anti-dispensationalists to the teaching of Scripture. While they admit that many of us who oppose them believe just as fervently as they in the inerrancy of Scripture, they think they are humbler in accepting its straightforward teaching. We tend to be more sophisticated and less submissive. They are childlike in their faith; we are less so. They, to use the words of Isaiah, "tremble" more at God's Word than we do.

This difference in approach and attitude comes to the surface in dispensationalism's "literalism" versus our supposed "spiritualizing." Dispensationalists think they take the Bible at its word, whereas we make it conform to our anticipations. They are more literal, willing to follow the words of Scripture wherever they lead. We, they think, make the Scripture fit into our own pre-conceived theology. When its literal meaning does not fit, we must spiritualize it, whereas they remain faithful to its literal teaching.

While dispensationalists see themselves as literalists and their opponents as spiritualizers, their conservative opponents maintain that they are wrong on both counts. First, dispensationalists themselves are not consistent literalists, and, second, their opponents do not spiritualize unless they feel Scripture itself, taken literally, has a spiritual or metaphorical meaning. Both groups try to follow, consciously or unconsciously, the dictum of Martin Luther: "Literal wherever possible." As Radmacher has astutely observed, "Literalism is not letterism."

We all agree that most literature, including the Bible, is meant to be understood according to the literal construction of the words that are used. Even in common speech, we assume a person should be taken literally unless he is obviously using a metaphor, or is allegorizing, or is in some way alerting us that the usual meaning of his words is not in play at the moment. Then, and then only, will we interpret other than literally. The same is true with respect to the Bible.

But all literalists, at one point or another, interpret the Bible figuratively. There is not a dispensationalist living who believes that, when Christ said He was the vine, grapes were to be picked from His body. On the other hand, when our Lord said, "I am the way, the truth, and the life," no one doubts that He meant He was the only way anyone could come to the Father. That was no figure of speech but an absolute, literal, dogmatic statement that He was the only way to eternal life.

The vast proportion of Scripture is either obviously literal or obviously figurative, both sides admit. Only in a relatively few disputed areas does the question arise whether the Scripture is to be taken literally or figuratively. We do not accuse dispensationalists of being absolute literalists, nor should they accuse us of being absolute spiritualizers.

We both are literalists up to a certain point. At the points where we differ, dispensationalists generally interpret the passage literally, and non-dispensationalists, figuratively. But *to say on the basis of that limited divergence of interpretation that the two schools represent fundamentally different hermeneutical approaches is not warranted.* Many on both sides do think that this hermeneutical difference is more foundational than the theological. I profoundly disagree.

4

If the usual distinction between dispensationalists and non-dispensationalists as literalists and spiritualizers is not a valid one, what is the issue here? As I said above, it comes back to this matter of *dividing* the Word of God as over against *unifying* the Word of God. The dispensationalist sees in various periods diverse dispensations rather than a harmonious unfolding of different dispensations. In other words, the difference here is not so much in the fundamental hermeneutical approach as in the interpretations.

As the dispensationalist approaches prophecy, he does not differ from the non-dispensational conservative. They both believe they are addressing the Word of God; both have confidence in predictive prophecy; and both are endeavoring to understand what the Word of God means. But at this point the two interpretations diverge into a separation versus an integration of the parts of Scripture.

It is very difficult to say which is the cart and which is the horse in this case. Is it the literalistic tendency that produces this divided Scripture, or is it the belief in a divided Scripture that drives the dispensationalist to ultra-literalism at some point? I think it is the latter, though that is not easy to prove.

I let this matter rest for now. The remainder of this pamphlet will look at the divergent interpretations and, incidentally, at the way the two groups do interpretation and why. Here, it is sufficient to observe that the dispensationalist divides Scripture according to a common misconstruction of II Timothy 2:15, whereas the anti-dispensationalist, believing that is a misinterpretation of the text, sees an overriding unity in the Word of God.

APPLICATIONS OF THIS FUNDAMENTAL IDEA

This radical disparateness of the Bible is the fundamental motif of dispensationalists, and it manifests itself in crucial areas. First, I will consider the dispensational conception of the people of God. Second, I will note the dispensationalist's idea of the predestination of the people of God. Third, I will examine the dispensational view of the salvation of the people of God. Fourth, I will conclude with the dispensationalist's view of the future of the people of God.

Dispensationalism and the People of God

John Calvin referred to some proto-dispensationalists of the Reformation period as reducing Israel to "a herd of swine." The "dispensationalists" of the time regarded the ancient people of God as merely temporal. Their life was in this world and their hope was in this world. They were satisfied if they could sit in peace under their own fig tree with no invading foe troubling them. Temporal prosperity was their heaven, and they did not look far beyond.

Calvin thought otherwise. In his *Institutes of the Christian Religion,* he devotes an entire chapter, "The Similarity of the Old and New Testaments," to the *spiritual* interests of the Old Testament people of God. In essence, they were the same as the New Testament saints. Some individuals of the old dispensation exceeded spiritually many in the new dispensation. Calvin begins with these words and continues in the same vein throughout the chapter: ". . . it may now be evident that all those persons, from the beginning of the world, whom God has adopted into the society of his people, have been federally [convenantally] connected with him by the same law and the same doctrine which are in force among us."

Of course, dispensationalists do not refer to Israel as a "herd of swine." In fact, they resent such a description of their viewpoint. Nevertheless, they think of Israel as the "wife of Jehovah" in distinction from the New Testament people of God, who are described as the "bride of Christ." The wife of Jehovah would seem equivalent to the bride of Christ. Jehovah in the Old Testament is, of course, the Lord Jesus Christ.

Nevertheless, dispensationalists confine the Old Testament "wife of Jehovah" to earthly blessings, in distinction from the heavenly blessings of the "bride of Christ."

This division between the Old Testament people of God and the New Testament people of God is far-reaching. For example, it divides at the point of regeneration and new birth. To be a member of the New Testament people of God, one must be born of the Spirit. No matter how outwardly moral a person is, he is not saved and a member of the true church of Jesus Christ unless he is a new creature. By contrast, the Old Testament saint was not a born-again Christian. For example, Lewis Sperry Chafer says of Nicodemus that he was a perfected Jew under the Old Testament law. He was not born-again but a true Israelite. He was a genuine member of the Old Testament people of God though he, at that time, had not entered the company of the New Testament people of God. Dispensationalists see Paul, prior to his conversion, after the same model. Before his conversion, this Jew was "as touching the law, blameless." The dispensationalist takes this to mean that he met the Old Testament requirements. In that dispensation, he too was a "perfected Jew." Only when he was born again did he become a member of the church of Jesus Christ.

By contrast, the covenantal view of the people of God sees in both dispensations the same people of God. All are members of the church, all are born-again, and all are saved by the one mediator between God and man, the man, Christ Jesus. The same church of Jesus Christ comprises both. One is not a swinish, earthly people, and the other a regenerate, heavenly people. They are both the people of God, born of His Spirit, created anew by the Lord Jesus Christ.

The church, says Chafer-Walvoord, is "the body of Christ, . . . called out of the world and joined together with a living union in Christ. This concept is not found in the Old Testament . . ." (*Major Bible Themes,* p. 234). That is to say, the body of Christ did not exist in the Old Testament. The Old

Testament people of God were not called out of the world and joined together "with a living union in Christ." A dispensationalist will deny that this opens up the possibility of different ways of salvation; however one group has a living union with Christ and the other has none. A dispensationalist will say that all are saved by Jesus Christ, but they are not in living communion with Jesus Christ.

According to dispensationalists, there are three categories of people: (1) the Jew, (2) the Gentile, and (3) the church of God. The Jews, or Israel, are the descendants of Abraham and Jacob ("Israel") who have the earthly promises. (Abraham is said to have "spiritual" as well as temporal blessings but not regeneration, adoption, and "living union in Christ." He was the "channel" of such blessing but not the recipient himself.) These Jews are now scattered in the whole world and later will be gathered together. The church consists of those Jews and Gentiles who have been born again and are members of Jesus Christ. The Gentiles are the rest of mankind who never had any kind of acceptable relationship to God. In other words, dispensationalists see three categories where the Bible sees only two: the people of God and those who are not the people of God. There are those who are saved and those who are not saved. There are those who are in Christ and those who are not in Christ. But what God has joined together (Old and New Testament church), I fear dispensationalists have rent asunder. The one undivided church of all time the dispensationalist divides in two irreconcilable parts: the Jewish, Israelitish people of God and the Christian people of God. And the church is not only separated in this world but even in the world to come.

Abraham himself shows that the dispensational division between Israel and the church is erroneous. The Israelites descended from Abraham, but dispensationalists sever them, as well as Abraham himself, from the people in living union with Jesus Christ. Yet, in the New Testament, those who are in living union with Jesus Christ are the seed of Abraham. Christ Himself says to the Jews, "If you are Abraham's children, do the deeds of Abraham . . . . Your father Abraham rejoiced to see my day; and he saw it and was glad" (John 8:39, 56). According to our Lord, these lineal descendants of Abraham were not really the seed or children of Abraham at all since they did not come to living union with Jesus Christ. Those who have a living union with Jesus Christ are the true Israelites. So, we see that not all lineal descendants of Abraham were necessarily the children of Abraham, but only those lineal descendants of Abraham (as well as Gentiles) who came to Jesus Christ. The true children or descendants of Abraham and the Christian church are one and the same.

In Romans 4 Paul says the same thing—the children of faith are the children of Abraham. He himself was an Israelite, but he did not become a true child of Abraham until he became a believer, in union with Jesus Christ. In other words, the New Testament teaches that New Testament saints belong to the church by a living union with Jesus Christ, and as such, they are in union with the people of God in all dispensations who are the true children of Abraham.

Christ is much more visible in the New Testament, of course. Living union is much more apparent, but there is no denying, even by the dispensationalists, that Christ is the eternal Son of God and was very active in the Old Testament and that even the salvation of the Israelites rested on faith in Jesus Christ.

Dispensationalists cannot have it both ways. If the Old Testament people of God had no union with Christ, they were not saved by Him. If they were saved by Christ, dispensationalists have to admit that the Israel of the Old Testament and the church of the New are one and the same body of people, all of them in union with Jesus Christ and, as such, the true sons of Abraham. God has joined the people of God in all dispensations in Jesus Christ. Dispensationalists have divided them.

Predestination and the People of God

Dispensationalists are popularly known as "four point" Calvinists. Many people know the five points of Calvinism by the famous acrostic, *TULIP: T* = total depravity; *U* = unconditional election; *L* = limited atonement; *I* = irresistible grace; and *P* = perseverance of the saints. Most dispensationalists claim to believe all of these biblical doctrines except limited atonement. In other words, they believe in total depravity, election, irresistible grace, and the perseverance of the saints. I am not accusing my dispensational friends of dishonesty, but of not understanding the doctrines they profess. If they did understand them, they would realize that they disagree with all five and not merely with one.

For example, dispensationalists profess to believe in unconditional election. They say a great deal about the subject and intend to affirm this great truth of Holy Scripture. But what do dispensationalists mean by their affirmation of unconditional election?

The Scofield Bible note on I Peter 5:13 ("The Church that is at Babylon, elected together with you . . .") says that election is according to foreknowledge. It is unconditional *salvation* that dispensationalists are talking about. God foresees that the sinner will repent. Because God foresees this repentance and belief of the sinner, He chooses him to everlasting life without the sinner's having any virtue which recommends him for election. All of this is quite true. But it is not what *unconditional election* means. That doctrine teaches that God elects the sinner while he is in his sin before he even turns away from sin or turns to faith. *It is the election that is unconditional, not merely the resulting salvation.* If God chooses or elects a person, foreseeing his repentance and faith, that may well be an unconditional *salvation*, but it is not an unconditional *election.* (In fact it would not even be an unconditional *salvation* but salvation conditioned by a non-meritorious, necessary faith.)

Furthermore, dispensationalism repudiates Calvinism by its explicit rejection of the third point, limited atonement, and by its misinterpretation of the first point, total depravity.

The dispensationalist explicitly rejects limited atonement. The very fact that he rejects the doctrine that Jesus Christ died to secure the salvation of only the unconditionally elected shows that the dispensationalist does not believe in unconditional election. If election is unconditional (that is, of sinners indisposed ever to repent or believe so long as they remained in their sins) then the only ones to benefit from Christ's atoning sacrifice are people specifically called by the Holy Spirit and enabled to repent and believe. The atonement is limited by God's choice to save some sinners and not others. All of this is alien to the dispensational mind because the doctrine of unconditional election is not really there either. So, we say to the dispensationalist that *he ought to stop affirming the unconditional election of totally depraved persons or else stop denying the limited design of the atonement.* Since his denial of limited atonement is consistent with all of his teaching, he ought to see immediately that he cannot possibly affirm (consistently) the Calvinistic doctrine of unconditional election.

The dispensationalist also affirms total depravity. Again, I do not question his honesty; but I must deny his perceptiveness. How could a person believe that men are dead in trespasses and sins, that they hate God, are utterly indisposed to Christ, are totally depraved, and are morally unable to incline toward any virtue, least of all the virtue of coming to the spotless Lamb of God, and say in the next breath that God merely foresees these persons as repenting and believing? Corpses do not give birth to spiritual life. Men have to be unconditionally elected to repentance, faith, and the salvation Christ specifically purchased for them.

The dispensationalist has a genuine desire to honor the predestinating, electing grace of God. There are so many

11

passages in the Bible that affirm it, and dispensationalists are so biblical that inevitably they affirm it too. On the other hand, what the Bible means by the doctrine makes the dispensationalist uncomfortable. He cannot deny it because the words are in Scripture, but he cannot affirm it because the concept is not really acceptable to him.

The dispensationalist handles the problem by avoiding it. He gives lip-service to divine sovereignty and human freedom. He constantly reminds us that both are taught in the Bible and both must be honored, but how they can be in harmony with one another is an inscrutable mystery. All that is true, but it does not explain what the doctrine is. A predestination of some corpses to live and some corpses to remain dead is what is manifestly meant by the Bible doctrine. Mankind is a valley of dry bones. Some of those dry bones are destined to live again and others are not. We have a sea of drowning sinners. Some are chosen to be rescued; some are left to drown. It is all very plain, but is not very palatable. The dispensationalist, as well as everybody else, shrinks from having to say that God lets many persons perish and chooses to save only some of the multitude. While they will not deny the doctrine outright, neither will they unambiguously affirm it.

Dispensationalists say that God has a plan. He knows even apart from that plan (*Major Christian Doctrines,* p. 233) what will inevitably happen. He lets it happen. That is about as far as the dispensationalist will go. But, to be true to the Bible, he must assert that God chooses to regenerate some and not to regenerate others. The dispensationalist will not deny it, but neither will he assert it. He makes predestination rest on foreknowledge, although he will not assert that unambiguously either. The dispensationalist finds himself between a rock and a hard place. He is biblical enough to know the Reformed truth and to want to believe it, but he cannot screw up enough courage to affirm it unconfusedly and unambiguously. He ends up with Arminianism, but he will not categorically affirm that either.

If anything is characteristically associated with Calvinism, it is predestinarianism. Calvinists believe all the classic, fundamental tenets of the Christian religion, of course. But what distinguishes them in the popular, and even in the academic, mind is their strong affirmation of the predestinating, unconditional election of almighty God. If a dispensationalist wants to be known as essentially Calvinistic, he cannot give any uncertain sound on this doctrine. Actually, he sounds the wrong note, but this is so subdued that dispensationalists themselves hardly detect it. They need to be aware, however, that they are not clearly, articulately, and emphatically stating what the Reformed faith has maintained down through the ages.

A clear comment on this subject comes in the Scofield note on I Peter 1:20. There he maintained that the relationship between election and foreknowledge is logically, first, omniscience, and second, divine decision, which includes foreordination, election, predestination, and foreknowledge. Yet, this is another instance of the hopeless obscurity of the doctrine in the dispensational mind. That statement would be truly Calvinistic if it unambiguously said that the divine decision (foreordination, election, and predestination) logically precedes foreknowledge, and this note does indicate that. Unfortunately, that is not all it says. It lists at the head of the logical verities *omniscience*. So, the order is omniscience, predestination, foreknowledge. That adds up to confusion—pure, simple, and eternal confusion. Omniscience means the knowledge of everything. But how could God have logically prior knowledge of everything before he has logically predestinated anything?

Furthermore, how can omniscience not include foreknowledge? How can God have all-knowledge (omniscience) without foreknowledge (which dispensationalists represent as logically following on omniscience)? In other words, dispensationalists out-do typical Arminians here. Arminians erroneously teach that predestination logically follows foreknowledge, but even they do not make the further error of teaching that even foreknowledge logically follows omniscience. Foreknowledge, in the sense of prescience, is part of omniscience.

The first three doctrines of the five points go by the board in dispensational theology. It has no true doctrine of total depravity; it has no true doctrine of unconditional election; and it has no true doctrine of the specific design of the atonement. It is conscious only of the last deviation from the Reformed faith. I hope I have succeeded in making it conscious of the first two also. I pray that it will be consistent even if it has explicitly to repudiate all three great Reformed truths, but, rather than that, I hope that it will *consistently affirm* all three.

Dispensationalism rejects the other two of the five points as well. For example, Dallas Theological Seminary, which is the largest and most famous academic exponent of dispensationalism in the world, makes regeneration "come through" faith: "We believe that the new birth of the believer comes only through faith in Christ . . ." (1981-82 Catalogue, Article VII), whereas according to irresistible grace, faith "comes through" the new birth.

Not quite so explicitly, but clearly, Dallas repudiates the fifth point, the *perseverance* of the saints. The Catalogue, Article X, on "eternal security" shows that dispensationalism believes in the "security" of believers whether they "persevere" or not. When saints "persistently sin," God will "chasten them and correct them in infinite love; but having undertaken to save them and keep them forever, apart from all human merit, He, who cannot fail, will in the end present everyone of them faultless before the presence of His glory and conformed to the image of His Son." Sinners are secure even though they "persistently sin." This would be perseverance of the sinners, not perseverance of the saints.

Salvation and the People of God

Dispensationalism is not, as it usually claims to be, Calvinistic or Reformed. This is an extremely serious fault inasmuch as the teaching of the Bible, we believe, is Reformed throughout. Jesus Christ gave a mandate when He commissioned His church, to teach people to observe whatsoever He had commanded them (Matt. 28:20). He has commanded in the Old and the New Testament the teaching of the "whole counsel" of God, which is indeed the Reformed system of theology. For dispensationalism to deviate from that is a serious fault. To claim *not* to do so, while doing so, is an even more serious fault. Nevertheless, it is not a *fatal* fault. It is possible, *very inconsistently*, to preserve the Christian religion while taking away its systematic character. It is sinfully possible to be faithful to the heart of the gospel even while departing from the context of it. I would by no means minimize the gravity of such defection, though I believe it is not fatal.

But what is indisputably, absolutely, uncompromisingly essential to the Christian religion is its doctrine of salvation. While a theologian may depart from the Reformed system and travel at his own peril, to depart from the essential salvation pattern is to depart from Christianity. Consequently, the doctrine which we now consider is of the essence. If dispensationalism has actually departed from the only way of salvation which the Christian religion teaches, then we must say it has departed from Christianity. No matter how many other important truths it proclaims, it cannot be called Christian if it empties Christianity of its essential message. We define a sect or cult as a group of people who claim to be Christian while voiding the essential message. If dispensationalism does this, then dispensationalism is a cult and not a branch of the Christian church. It is impossible to exaggerate the gravity of this situa-

15

tion.

What then does dispensationalism teach about the people of God and salvation? Happily, I find that all dispensationalists of whom I have ever heard or read maintain with vigor and emphasis that they believe that Jesus Christ is the only Savior in *all* dispensations. The cross of Christ is the way of justification for *everyone* from Adam to the last saint who will ever be saved. No matter how things appear on the surface, they insist that, at the bottom, the blood of Christ is the only ground of salvation for anybody at any time.

Our dispensational friends emphatically affirm their adherence to the essential Christian way of salvation. Whatever their intentions may be, they nonetheless fail to carry them out in their theology. However frequently they affirm their loyalty to the indispensable way of salvation in the blood of Jesus Christ, their system of doctrine relentlessly militates against this.

They do not grasp that point, and I honor them for sincerely opposing my charge. But, they cannot consistently maintain that opposition while teaching their system of doctrine. They must *face this criticism fairly. Unless they can show some fallacy in it, they must repudiate the dispensational system or else repudiate the gospel of Jesus Christ.* It cannot be placed in any less grim light than that. I admit my own fallibility. I am open to all counter-criticism. I have been waiting for years to see a dispensationalist refute that proposition and demonstrate not only that he *intends* to glory in the cross but that he actually *does* while maintaining the dispensational system of theology. He has not done this so far. I am afraid that he cannot do so. Many people will vigorously and indignantly reject this charge without even considering, much less weighing, it. That is not worthy of a Christian; what is appropriate at this point is either to refute or to recant. Rejection and repudiation of me is no substitute. Let the dispensationalist hear me fairly; then, let him submit to this criticism and abandon this false theology or attempt to refute it. Let him hear my response, and let us *all*

16

follow where the truth leads. As God is my witness, if I see myself to be wrong, I will acknowledge it, beg forgiveness of all dispensationalists, correct my ways, and humbly teach the truth, the whole truth, and nothing but the truth.

Why do I say that the dispensational system is against the cross of Jesus Christ, which it professes to exalt? First, the dispensational distinction between Israel and the church implies a different way of salvation. Second, their very concept of predestination also implies a different way of salvation. Third, the very meaning of the term, "dispensationalism," rules out the possibility of the Christian way of salvation. Fourth, their notion of the kingdom being offered by Jesus Christ, which, if accepted, would have made the cross unnecessary, is incompatible with the Christian way of salvation. Fifth, their view of the Old Testament people of God trusting in the coming of Christ rather than in the coming Christ is a fatal error. Sixth, and by far the most important incompatible element in the dispensational system, is its antinomianism, which precludes the possibility of the Christian way of salvation.

First, the dispensational distinction between Israel and the church implicitly repudiates the Christian way of salvation. Dispensationalists make a qualitative distinction between Israel and the church. They are two different peoples, not the same people of God. They have a different relationship to Him in this life and a different future.

If these are two different types of people, how can they have the same salvation? If, as dispensationalists maintain, Israel as well as the church is saved by the blood of Jesus Christ, how can there be this qualitative difference between them as peoples? Jesus Christ is the same yesterday, today, and forever. His salvation is the same yesterday, today, and forever. It may be administered in somewhat different ways, or different contexts, but what is administered is the same: redemption by the blood of Jesus Christ. The whole church has taught down through the centuries, and even the dispensationalists profess to believe, that there cannot be two different categories of people. How can those who are saved in the same way, by the same Savior, through the same redemption be a different people? How can Israel be reduced to a "herd of swine" and at the same time be the beneficiaries of the same blood of Christ from which we present-day Christians benefit?

It will not do to say that Israelites were the beneficiaries of the same redemption if they benefit in an entirely different manner. According to dispensationalists, the Old Testament people are not the heirs of the Holy Spirit and are not regenerated and grafted by Him into Christ in the same way that the New Testament people are. If Christ purchased the same thing for the Old Testament saints before He came that He did for the New Testament saints after He came, there cannot be a qualitative difference between them. There being clearly that difference, as the dispensationalists *vigorously maintain,* then there must be what the dispensationalists *vigorously deny,* a different basis of their acceptability with God.

The Bible teaches that the people of God are the same in all dispensations. They are, as Ephesians 2:20 says, built on the same foundation, "the prophets and apostles." The prophets of the Old Testament and the apostles of the New Testament are together a foundation for the church of God. The apostle Peter uses the same language for the New Testament church of God that was used for the ancient people of God in the Old Testament, calling them a royal priesthood and a holy nation: "But ye are a chosen generation, a royal priesthood, a holy nation, a people of his own, that ye should show forth the praises of him who hath called you . . ." (I Pet. 2:9).

In Paul's famous metaphor, the Jews were the original olive tree into which the Gentile believers were grafted (Rom. 11:17f.). They are the same plant; they have the same source of life; there is no difference between them except a temporal one. The early form of organization was displaced by the present form of organization, but the living stock of their lives,

Jesus Christ, is the same in all periods. The Bible says this because it maintains what the dispensationalist only claims, namely, that Christ is the one and only Savior of all time. It does not split the church, as dispensationalists do, but unifies the church in all ages because it sees that they are all saved by the same undivided Lord Jesus Christ.

Second, the dispensationalists' doctrine of predestination eliminates a sound doctrine of salvation. This is not so obvious as the first point, but it is equally true and can be demonstrated (with some difficulty) just as clearly.

If salvation comes to the individual by virtue of his foreseen faith, then, of course, his salvation is not the same as that which comes by God's predestinating grace. The salvation that comes to a mortally sick person who can at least reach out and take and apply the medicine that cures him is a very different thing from the salvation that comes to a corpse. Dispensational thought, growing out of the defection from the predestinarianism of the Bible, means that the sinner is still, though barely, alive. He can be restored to health by the exercise of his own weakened, but not destroyed, abilities. He is not saved by grace alone. He is saved by the offer of grace appropriated by his own remaining moral ability. Christ does not save him but makes salvation possible for him. Surely there is a vast difference between Christ as an aid to a person's salvation and Christ as the person's salvation. It is true that the dispensationalist will consistently say that a sinner cannot be saved without Christ, but that remnant of the gospel in their message is not the whole gospel. The gospel is not that Christ makes salvation possible but that He makes it actual. He is not a potential but a real Savior of His people from their sins.

The dispensationalist really says that the sinner in his present condition is still acceptable to God. God will reject sinners if they do not take steps toward God, but they still have the power to do that, and, if they do what is in their power, they will, by coming to Christ, save themselves. *Christ enables people to save themselves.* They initiate that act of salvation by appropriating the divine remedy offered in Jesus Christ. The dispensationalist will be outraged by this; he does not realize what he says because he puts so much verbal stress on the divinity of the remedy and the indispensability of the offer of the gospel. He cannot remain blind, however, to the conclusion that the sinner himself has it in his power to take this medicine, and, if he does take it, he most certainly (by applying Christ to himself) saves himself. It is perfectly clear to the dispensationalist that, without Christ, he could not save himself. He would certainly die apart from the rescue offered by Jesus Christ. Nevertheless, Christ alone does not save the sinner; the sinner appropriates the offer of Christ; the sinner is the decisive one.

As an illustration, suppose there are twins in a given Christian family. They are reared by the same godly father and mother and, in very young years, introduced to the same gospel of Jesus Christ. They are convicted of their sinfulness and their need of a Savior and also that salvation has been offered in Jesus' blood and righteousness. One of these twins embraces the gospel, which his parents present, and the other refuses to do so. The one who believes will be saved; the one who disbelieves will be lost. According to the dispensationalist, both of the boys have it in their power to believe Jesus Christ or to disbelieve Jesus Christ. The one brother believes Him; the other brother disbelieves Him. The one brother thus brings everlasting salvation to himself; the other brother brings everlasting damnation to himself. When we ask Paul's question, "Who has made you to differ?," we do not get the answer that the apostle Paul calls for. "For who maketh thee to differ from another? And what hast thou that thou didst not receive? Now if thou didst receive it, why dost thou glory, as if thou hadst not received it?" (I Cor. 4:7).

Clearly it is God who makes these persons to differ. Dispensationalists disagree. It is clearly the twins, not God. God is the same to both of them. Christ has died alike for each of them.

The gospel is offered in the same terms to both boys. The difference between them is not God or Christ. The difference is within themselves. One exercises faith; the other one does not. The one saves himself by believing in Christ; the other one damns himself by disbelieving in Christ. But it is the person himself, and not the Lord Jesus Christ or the sovereign God, who causes them to differ.

Think of Jacob and Esau. How does Paul talk about those biblical twins? "[For the children being not yet born, neither having done any good or evil, that the purpose of God according to election might stand, not of works, but of him that calleth], It was said unto her, the elder shall serve the younger. As it is written, Jacob have I loved, but Esau have I hated" (Rom. 9:11-13). Jacob and Esau differ because the sovereign God loved Jacob and hated Esau. He made Jacob a vessel of mercy and left Esau to be a vessel of wrath.

A dispensationalist cannot say that. He would sooner choke than glory in himself; however, insofar as he is a dispensationalist, *he does not glory in the cross but in his own acceptance of the cross.* If this offends him, then thank God it offends him, because it means that in his heart he believes what by his mind he disavows. Let him bring his mind in line with his heart. It will never do for him to say that, in his heart, he trusts in Christ alone as the author as well as the finisher of his salvation when he himself is the author of his salvation (and ultimately even the finisher of it). If he really believes God is the author, then let him say so. That, I believe, will be the end of his dispensationalism.

Third, the very meaning of the term "dispensation" militates against the Christian gospel of salvation. The definition of "dispensation" according to the revised Scofield Bible is a period when persons are tested with reference to their "obedience to some specific revelation of the will of God" (Gen. 1:28). A person is acceptable or unacceptable to God by the way he behaves with respect to certain commandments in certain ages. Construed literally, this is a form of justification or salvation by works.

The dispensationalist will recoil from this charge. He will answer that Christ is the underlying basis of salvation in all dispensations. But if that is so, why does the dispensationalist say that a person is tested with respect to his conscience or his observance of government or the law or something else? If the dispensationalist replies, ''This is just a test of his sincerity and the reality of his faith,'' well and good. He immediately ceases to be a dispensationalist and becomes a covenant theologian. He cannot throw this in as a sop to satisfy his critics; he must articulate it. ''Dispensation'' is his fundamental concept. But while I read many statements about dispensations, I never read that all these tests are simply to show that a person is really trusting in Jesus Christ. If he did say that, the dispensationalist would have to say that these tests apply in all dispensations. That is, a Christian individual must always honor his enlightened conscience; he must always respect those in authority; he must even observe the various ecclesiastical laws of God (as the dispensationalist does say). But, what difference would there be between one dispensation and another except the clarity of unfolding revelation? Why would there be different economies of redemption if the one covenant of grace underlay all of them? Why would these dispensational theologians not insist that they are indeed *covenant* theologians and that these dispensational differences are only what the Reformed theologians of the ages have been calling ''modal'' (not essential) differences. The essence of all dispensations is salvation by grace in the shed blood of Jesus Christ. That is what covenant theologians say and build their theology on. That is what dispensational theologians say, but they erect their theology on an entirely different foundation.

Dispensationalism *per se* denies covenantism at the same time that dispensationalists defend themselves from that charge by surreptitiously suggesting that they are covenant theologians. They do not use this language, but when we criticize them for offering differing schemes of salvation, they say, "No, it is the same way; it is the same covenant; it is the same shed blood of Jesus Christ." If they are going to say that conscientiously, then they must stop saying the other. If they are going to say the other, it will not do to make this evangelical gesture, which is incompatible with the fundamental concept of dispensationalism.

Still, the dispensationalist does *not* say, strictly speaking, that Christ is the Savior in all dispensations. This most definitive Scofield note on "dispensation" explicitly *rejects* Christ in what is meant to affirm Him. According to that note, there are *not* separate ways of salvation. But why? Because, even before the cross, man was "saved in prospect of Christ's atoning sacrifice," *accordingly, those before the cross were not saved by "believing on the Lord Jesus Christ" but "in prospect of Christ's sacrifice."* There is an infinite difference between being saved by Christ's sacrifice and being *saved in "prospect"* of it! If a dispensationalist replies that I am quibbling with language, he cannot be in earnest. That difference in the ways of salvation is the most crucial difference between the two theologies. If a dispensationalist gives up that distinction, he gives up his dispensationalism!

I do sense a trend among dispensationalists back to the orthodoxy from which they have departed. Even the differences between the revised Scofield Bible of 1967 and the original Scofield of the turn of the century show the revisers moving away from the older dispensationalism toward the more orthodox, Reformed theology. Nevertheless, I have to say that, though they may be moving in the right direction, they have not *departed* from the older, seriously defective doctrine. I pray with all my heart that this movement in the right direction will carry them back to where they belong—with us in the Reformed faith. But, until then, I cannot withdraw my criticism that this is another gospel, which is not another gospel. I am not saying they *intend* everything that they say and write. Nevertheless, as teachers in the church, they must teach soundly. They cannot excuse error on the ground that they *mean* truth. If they mean the truth in their hearts, then they must express it by their lips. It is out of the heart that either sin or righteousness proceeds, as our Lord says. He sees the heart; we creatures can only hear the mouth. This is no doubt the reason Paul insists that *"if you confess with your mouth* Jesus as Lord, and believe in your heart that God raised Him from the dead, you shall be saved"* (Rom. 10:9).

If in his heart the dispensationalist loves the gospel and believes that it is the same in all ages and that all people are always saved only by that one way, let him say so consistently and repudiate everything in his system that is inconsistent.

He should not need any vigorous exhortation at this point. If he truly loves the gospel of Jesus Christ and considers this criticism fair and is incapable of refuting it, then surely he will thank us, repudiate his error, embrace the truth, and be one with us in the covenant theology of the ages.

Fourth, the dispensationalists' conception of an offer of the kingdom which could have made the cross unnecessary is an appalling, implicit rejection of the gospel. In dispensational thinking of the most moderate character, Jesus Christ came to offer an earthly kingdom to Israel. That kingdom would have fully established the Old Testament legal system, and its expansion through the whole world under the leadership of a revived Israel and her Messiah. All the errors that belong to the dispensational conception of the age of the law would have been reenacted at that time had Israel accepted their king, Jesus. Fortunately, for the dispensationalist and all of us, the Jews rejected Christ's supposed offer and doomed Him to the cross. Christ's death on the cross, which came about only because Israel did not accept Him as the king of Israel, is the basis of our salvation in this dispensation of grace, or the age of the church. In other words, the gospel was a happy accident for Christians. It depended entirely on the faithlessness of the Jews. Had they responded as they ought to have responded, there would never have been a gospel of Jesus Christ. This is surely an appalling notion. How a Christian could entertain it, even momentarily, is very difficult to understand.

Dispensationalists account for such an appalling concept by their view of divine sovereignty. They say that God knew from all eternity that, when the Jews were presented with the kingdom by the Lord Christ, they would refuse it. Consequently, Christ could not have set up His kingdom at that time, thus making the cross unnecessary. Many of them say they are as shocked by the implication that the cross of Christ might never have occurred as we are. But they are tranquil because God knew that this would never happen.

Ironically, dispensationalists think they are very Calvinistic at this point. God does know all things and, in a certain sense, foreordains all things. They rest in that Calvinistic doctrine to free themselves from any guilt in teaching this incredible notion that the cross was, strictly speaking, unnecessary. "No, it was necessary," they insist. God knew that it *had to* take place. And God knew that it *would* take place because He knew that the Jews would not accept this offer which would have made the cross unnecessary.

God was offering Israel a very, very, very wicked option. According to dispensationalism, the Lord Jesus Christ offered something to the Jews in good faith which, had they accepted, would have destroyed the only way of man's salvation. God is an honest God. He is a sincere God. He, therefore, truly offered the Jews a kingdom which would have made the cross impossible. Now, obviously, if God did offer a kingdom which He could not have permitted to be established, He could be neither honest nor sincere. The dispensationalist tries to think that God was both honest and sincere because He *knew* the way in which people would respond to the offer. He was doing it safely, as it were, because He knew that this dishonest and in-

25

sincere offer would never be accepted. *The fact of the matter is He could not possibly have redeemed His promise had it been accepted.* If the Jews had embraced Christ's offer, God would have had to say, "I am sorry, Christ cannot be elevated to the throne at this time. He must die on a cross." If the Jews expostulated and said, "But you offered us this," He would have had to say that it was not a sincere offer. "I thought that you would never accept it." Of course, the dispensationalist in the background is saying, "No, that would never happen because God knew it would never happen." I am granting that it never could have happened. Still, the supposed offer was insincere. God was making an offer that He could never have redeemed, though *He dishonestly implied that He would if it were accepted.*

Dispensationalists counterattack at this point with considerable cogency because this is so highly hypothetical. They insist that what they are saying is no different from the Calvinistic interpretation of the "offer of the gospel." God knows who will and who will not accept it. The dispensationalist says to the Calvinist, "Suppose a person whom God had left to perish had chosen actually to believe. Could God have accepted that person's faith?" Would He not have said, "No, you were not chosen; therefore, you cannot have this gospel which you profess"? He could not have redeemed His promise. He offers it to everybody and if everybody actually were to accept it, then God could not actually save everybody, because He had already declared that everyone would not be saved. If He were to save everybody, He would prove Himself to be ignorant of what was going to happen and frustrated in all of His counsels and purposes. "So what difference is there," the dispensationalist asks, "between our saying that God knew that the Jews would reject the kingdom and make the cross necessary, and your saying that God knew that certain persons would reject Jesus Christ and thereby make His predestination and foreknowledge true so that He would not have to make good on His insincere offer of salvation?''

Clearly, the whole gospel goes if God can lie. If His promise is not ''Yea'' and ''Amen,'' we can never be persuaded that His offer of the gospel is genuine. The dispensationalist asks, ''If we fall, do you not fall with us?'' We answer, No! The dispensational representation of Reformed theology is a caricature at this point. We admit that, *if* we were guilty of what dispensationalists charge, our error *would be as fatal* as theirs. But, dispensationalists do not understand what we teach. We do not teach that God invites reprobates to believe and be saved, knowing full well that He will not give them a heart of faith. In fact, *God does not call reprobates!* Whom does He call? Sinners! Only those who recognize themselves to be sinners, are called. *Any one* of them who comes will be saved. *God never invited anyone who, if he responded, would be refused.* God would never be embarrassed, even hypothetically, by someone's coming and being rejected because he was not predestinated and foreknown. No one has been refused, would be refused, will be refused, ever.

Even Reformed theologians sometimes state this ''universal call'' incorrectly as if Christ were inviting the ''righteous'' to repentance.

However, according to Reformed theology, the call of the gospel is universally to all who are conscious of being ''sinners,'' ''poor in spirit,'' aware of needing a Savior. It never was or will be offered to the ''righteous,'' proud in spirit, and self-sufficient. So Christ makes no insincere invitation to persons He would not accept if they did come (which is precisely what dispensational teaching says He does in reference to offering His kingdom to the Jews).

It is true that our Lord said that many were called but few were chosen, as if only a few of those sincerely invited were accepted when they came, if they came. What Christ was saying was that the call went everywhere, but only those who paid attention to the nature of that call and came running were chosen

27

and were choosing. The self-righteous recognized that the call was not for them but for despised "sinners"—they did not choose and they were not chosen.

Fifth, the way dispensationalists conceive of the Old Testament believers is drastically different from the biblical way. According to dispensationalists, the Old Testament people are saved by believing *in the coming* of Christ while, in the biblical view, the Old Testament people are saved by believing *in the Christ* who is coming. *In dispensationalism, a person is saved by anticipation; in the biblical system, a person is saved by Christ.* If Christ is the only way of salvation in all dispensations, then in all dispensations, persons must be saved by Jesus Christ and not by an anticipation of His coming.

This is no artificial distinction. The Old Testament people are not saved by Jesus Christ, according to dispensationalism; they are saved by hope in the coming of Christ. As such, they do not benefit from what Christ actually achieves when He comes. They are not regenerated; their hopes are not heavenly; they are an earthly "herd of swine." Another way of salvation connected with Christ but not resting on Christ is indeed a different way. The dispensationalist at this point is, unconsciously perhaps, consistent. He does not regard the Old Testament people of God as second, third, or fourth class citizens, but they do not belong to the kingdom of God. They are not in the heavenlies with Christ Jesus. That is consistent with their not being saved by Jesus Christ, but it is inconsistent with being saved by Jesus Christ as the dispensationalists are always *saying*, while constantly, *by their doctrine, denying*.

Sixth, the antinomianism of dispensationalism is utterly incompatible with the one gospel of our Lord Jesus Christ. Dispensational theology does not honor the one way of salvation in other dispensations than the present one. It does not even honor the gospel of Jesus Christ *in this so-called dispensation of grace or of the church. This is the dispensation in which the gospel is supposed to come into its glory; but in this very dispensation it becomes most patently obvious that the dispensational gospel is another gospel altogether.* Antinomianism is anti-gospelism. One cannot be antinomian and Christian at the same time. If dispensationalists do not want to be anti-Christian, they must repudiate the antinomianism which is a part of the *warp and woof* of their "gospel."

Is dispensationalism truly antinomian? Antinomianism is the doctrine that a Christian is saved without any obligation to keep the law. "Apart from the law," in the antinomian mind, means apart from *any necessary* relation to the law. Their doctrine teaches that we are saved by faith alone. The usual way of stating Reformation doctrine is that we are "justified by faith alone but not by the faith that is alone." That is, we are justified by our union with Jesus Christ by true faith, but that faith is not alone because it bears the fruit of good works. Antinomians say that justification is by faith alone and by a faith that may be alone. The faith ought to bring forth good works but, if it does not, that is not fatal to faith. The antinomian will never put it this way, but it amounts to justification by a faith without works, justification by a "dead" faith. James says plainly that faith without works is "dead." If faith may exist without works in antinomianism, then that justification may be by a dead faith, that is, by no faith at all. Therefore, this denies the gospel of justification by faith and repudiates Christianity.

Dispensationalism is inseparably connected with antinomianism. Dispensationalism teaches that justification may occur by a dead faith. It is, therefore, an enemy of the central doctrine of the Christian religion—justification by faith alone. It is a champion of possible justification by no faith at all, since it maintains that *may* occur. It does not recommend that it *ought* to occur.

Dispensationalists, in their opposition to the law, are not, however, totally opposed to it. They recommend the keeping of the law—the moral law, the Christian law. They maintain that a person who believes himself to be saved by Christ ought to live for Christ. There is even a promise that, *if* he abounds in the work of the Lord, he will have a great reward. If, on the other hand, his faith is sterile, he will not enjoy *fellowship* with God. He will not be rejected by God, but neither will he be in happy communion with God. He is on his way to heaven, but he will not be happy along the way.

Some years ago, I was teaching a survey of church history to the staff members at Campus Crusade's summer Institute of Biblical Studies in Fort Collins, Colorado. Several times in the survey course, antinomianism was mentioned. One day, one of the members of that class came up to me and said, "Dr. Gerstner, will you read this chapter of Dr. Ryrie's and tell the class whether you think it is a modern expression of antinomianism?" I read that book of Dr. Ryrie's on Christian discipleship and particularly examined the chapter in question. The next day, I said to the class, "This is modern antinomianism." I was very sorry to see that my friend, Dr. Ryrie, was guilty of this awful doctrine, and, since there were several of his students in the class, I urged them to relay to Dr. Ryrie my deep distress and concern about this unsound teaching in this particular book. I knew of this trend in dispensationalism. I must admit, however, that I had never looked at it so carefully and been so thoroughly persuaded that this doctrine was taught even by one of dispensationalism's very best theologians, Charles Ryrie.

Those students did not relay my message to Dr. Ryrie, as I discovered when I met him in person a couple of years later in Chicago. We had only time there for a 15-minute conversation. During that conversation, Dr. Ryrie convinced me of one thing: he did not mean to be antinomian. I told him how happy I was of that. It assured me of what I thought was the case. At the same time, I said to him that his assurances did not convince me that he was not teaching the doctrine, but only that he did not mean to teach the doctrine. So, we agreed to carry on a further correspondence.

Shortly after I returned home, I received a copy of Dr. Ryrie's book on *Grace* with a number of passages underlined, all of which were meant to indicate how anti-antinomian Dr. Ryrie was. I wrote him a letter of appreciation for his intention to avoid this fatal error. I saw why he thought he had avoided it and why he thought these statements to which he had directed my attention supported his opposition to that doctrine. I spelled out to him in that five-page letter, that they did *not* succeed in doing what he thought they did. They did not prove that he was not antinomian. I gently charged him once again with antinomianism and hoped that he would carry on the correspondence proving to me that I was mistaken and that actually he was an opponent of this fatal error.

A couple of years have gone by now, and Dr. Ryrie has not answered my letter. When someone proposed that we have a two-and-a-half day public discussion on this subject, he declined that also. I am left with the unhappy conclusion that Dr. Ryrie is an antinomian who does not think he is an antinomian and does not feel it necessary to try to prove to me that he is innocent of the charge. I am very sorry about this, because I have to say about my friend that he is an unsound teacher of this dreadful error.

As an example of antinomian teachers I cite one of dispensationalism's most able expositors, Dr. Alvin McClain, a reviser of the Scofield Bible. I can do no better than examine his thoughtful little book entitled, *Law and Grace* (1967). He acutely argues that the New Testament expression "under the law" could have only one of two meanings. It referred to being under the law either as the basis of salvation or as a way of life. Since no one was ever, in any age, saved by keeping the law, the former possibility is excluded and the expression can only refer to being "under the law" as a way of life. So, when the New Testament says, as in Roman 6:14, that the Christian is not "under the law," it means that he is free from it as a way of life or standard of duty.

Dr. McClain's mistake is certainly not in the sharpness of his reasoning. What then? He assumes that, although the *Bible* never taught that the law was the basis of salvation, the Jews did not so misconstrue the Bible. That is precisely what they did. For example, the rich young ruler thought that he had "kept" the law from his youth up (Matt. 19:20). Paul himself had thought that, before his conversion, he had been "touching the righteousness which is in the law, blameless" (Phil. 3:6). The Pharisees and Jews generally trusted in their own righteousness as keepers of the law (Luke 18:9; Rom. 10:3). That "righteousness" is what, as a Christian, Paul found to be "dung," though he had cherished it before. So, in Romans 6:14, he says we are not "under the law" precisely in that sense. He saw that, when the Galatians had sought to be "justified by the law," they had, as it were, "fallen from grace" (Gal. 5:4). Consequently, Paul said that his doctrine "established" the (moral) law as the way of life—not as the meritorious ground for salvation. What Paul's doctrine of grace established, McClain's doctrine of grace destroyed. "Do we then make void the law through faith?" asks Paul. McClain answers, Precisely! Paul answers, "God forbid!" (Rom. 3:31).

The Future of the People of God

The doctrine of the future is the best known element in dispensational theology, and at the same time, the least important. Ten million people have bought copies of Hal Lindsey's *Late Great Planet Earth*. John Walvoord's *Armageddon* has sold more than 100,000 copies. These themes interest people concerned with world politics, the Near East, OPEC problems, etc. I think dispensationalism is consistently wrong in this area, but my real concern is not with their eschatological opinions but the underlying concept. That underlying concept is the difference between Israel and the church.

Most dispensationalists project this division between the people of God into all eternity. Israel is going to be a "herd of swine" for evermore. Her destiny is to be restored to a perfect condition on earth, everlastingly.

This is a classical instance of gaining the whole world and losing one's soul. Israel will gain the whole world but will lose its soul as the true Israel of God. This false distinction between the two peoples of God is projected endlessly.

This alone would be a total liability in dispensational theology. It is impossible everlastingly to divide the one people of God. The church is one in all ages. Those redeemed by the blood of Jesus Christ are the one body of Jesus Christ. That olive tree is the same olive tree. All the redeemed will come to sit down with Abraham, Isaac, and Jacob, as Jesus says. There is but one royal priesthood, one holy nation in all ages. Whatever differences there may be in time and condition under which the people of God live, they are reunited in the world to come, everlastingly one in the divine presence of the glorious redeemer of God's elect of all ages.

Only a difference in the way of salvation could justify this eternal division. It is incredible that the same body of people, redeemed by the same blood of Jesus Christ, should be perpetually separate from one another. If the church's one foundation is Jesus Christ her Lord, as the hymn says, she is one in heaven and on earth.

This eschatological concept is fundamental to dispensationalism, and the rapture is the most significant event on the eschatological calendar. Dispensationalists are full of this doctrine. We hear about it constantly. It is expected momentarily.

What is the rapture but the catching up of the church from the world into the heavenlies with Christ Jesus there to dwell with Him forevermore? According to dispensationalism, it is the prelude to the conversion of Israel and its glorified condition on earth. It is the prelude to the kingdom of heaven established in this world where the Jews are the servants of the Messiah and the proclaimers of His gospel in an earthly, legal form to the whole world. This "seventieth week" of Daniel is the burden of the whole last book of the Bible, the Revelation. There is contact with the past in the opening chapters and a reference to the eternal future of the church in heaven in the closing chapters; but chapters 4 to 20 of Revelation are concerned with the seventieth week of Daniel, the ultimate restoration of Israel and the Davidic kingdom of heaven. Almost the last thing that God does in His Word is make this unfortunately conceived distinction between Israel and the church permanent. Dividing the people of God is the last great "redemptive" act in which the Almighty engages, according to this unfortunate view.

I am not concerned here with eschatological details. To be absorbed in the details of Daniel's seventieth week while ignoring the fact that the interpretation splits the church of God through all eternity is pathetic, to say the least. Without any verse-by-verse refutation, it is obvious that any such interpretation is false. God clearly teaches that there is one Savior of God's elect in all ages. Any interpretation that obscures this is false. Jesus Christ's second coming is not to separate the church from the church, followed by a third coming to bring an end of the world. Without even looking at a single dispensational commentary in detail, it is perfectly obvious that a commentary which makes that out of the last book of the Bible is wrong—just as a liberal interpretation of the Bible which reduces Christ to the status of a man and His gospel to works-salvation is false; we need not bother with the details of its errors. Dispensationalists and non-dispensationalists alike know that anyone who reduces Christ to the status of a man and salvation to the status of human endeavor has not grasped the elemental details of the gospel. He may have all sorts of insights and wisdom about this, that, and the other detail; but he has missed the main message of the Bible. So then, whatever devotion dispensationalists have to the Bible and with whatever knowledge they adorn their comments, they fundamentally misunderstand the Bible. If they make it lead up to a climactic separation of the body of Jesus Christ, which He has purchased with His own blood and unified in Himself for all eternity, they have not so learned Christ.

CONCLUSION

Although dispensationalism has been the instrument of my salvation, its message, though well intended, destroys the salvation message. It tears my heart to say this because dispensationalism has meant so much to me and multitudes of others in another context. Nevertheless, I believe that this primer proves that charge.

Dispensationalism divides rather than preserves the unity of the Bible. It divides the people of God. It divides predestination from the people of God. It divides salvation from the people of God. It divides the people of God into the endless future. These things are incompatible with a sound interpretation of the Bible. If nothing more than this is said, I believe this proves that dispensationalism is not a biblical doctrine but is, in fact, anti-biblical at its essential level. Those who would like to study the matter more thoroughly may wish to consult the brief bibliography I have appended. I can only say to my dispensational friends, from the depth of my heart, "Please, unless you think you can refute this, acknowledge its truth. Repudiate this system of doctrine and soundly articulate the gospel you love and to which your life is devoted."

The reader may very well wonder how a person can attack as un-Christian a system of doctrine that has been the means of his own salvation. The explanation is fairly simple. There is enough truth in the dispensational system that a person understanding that truth apart from the rest of the system could very well be saved by it. Dispensationalism clearly teaches that the blood of Christ is the theme of the Bible throughout. In that, dispensationalism is absolutely correct. God used a dispensationalist dean in my conversion; from this teacher I learned that Christ's redemption is the central theme of the Bible and that redemption is essentially in the shedding of His blood. That was dispensationalism's contribution to me, and for that, I will be everlastingly grateful.

The dispensational system of doctrine, however, militates against that very emphasis. It actually vitiates the biblical doctrine of redemption by Jesus Christ; one can no longer trust in Jesus Christ alone as his Savior. In spite of all their declarations to the contrary, I have shown that dispensationalist make the cross of Christ of no effect. It is *obvious* that it is of no saving effect in the whole *Old Testament* economy and in the anticipated *kingdom*. I have also made it evident that, because antinomianism is the essence of dispensational understanding of the age of grace, dispensationalism even vitiates the cross in this period in which we now live. So, the dispensational system of theology is against the work of Jesus Christ in the Old Testament, in the New Testament, and in the kingdom of the world to come.

Just as truly as I was converted by hearing about the blood of Jesus from dispensational lips, so many of you may likewise have been converted under similar circumstances. Just as I came to learn that the blood of Christ was not really glorified in the dispensational system and thus to oppose the dispensational system, so I trust the same thing will be true of the reader. You may very well, for the rest of your lives, be grateful that you first came to know about Jesus Christ through some dispensational teacher or writing. If you learn properly about Jesus Christ, you will realize that those individuals who first brought the knowledge of Him to you actually undermine that knowledge in their full system of doctrine. So, grateful for the elemental truths (which come *in* their system though vitiated *by* their system), you can best show your gratitude by opposing them when they, thereafter, attack what they themselves declare. Just as I feel I am returning a debt of gratitude to dispensationalists for the truths which they do proclaim, by opposing the erroneous system in which they proclaim them, so I trust that you may do the same.

May it be with them as it was with Apollos whom Paul taught "a more excellent way." Whatever his error was, he was himself a true believer who, when shown a more excellent way, did not combat it but believed it and became a consistent Christian teacher and preacher of the gospel. May all dispensationalists readily embrace this more excellent way and propagate it with a purified zeal born from above.

BIBLIOGRAPHY

Dispensational Works:

Chafer, L. S. *Systematic Theology,* 8 vols. Dallas: Dallas Seminary Press, 1947-48.

_____ . *Major Bible Themes.* Revised by John F. Walvoord. Grand Rapids: Zondervan Publishing House, 1981.

Covenantal Works:

Allis, O. T. *Prophecy and the Church.* Phillipsburg, New Jersey: Presbyterian and Reformed Publishing Company, 1945.

Bass, C. *Backgrounds to Dispensationalism.* Grand Rapids: Eerdmans, 1960.

Calvin, J. *The Institutes of the Christian Religion,* Book II, Chapters X, XI.

Kevin, E. F. *The Grace of Law.* Grand Rapids: Baker Book House, 1965.

Warfield, B. B. Review of L. S. Chafer, *He That Is Spiritual* in *Princeton Theological Review* 17, 2 (April, 1919): 322-27.